I0759633

better together*

* This book is best read together, grownup and kid.

a
kids
book
about

a kids book about

by Jackson Cooper

A Kids Co.
Editor Emma Wolf
Designer Rick DeLucco
Head of Design Rick DeLucco
CEO and Founder Jelani Memory
Author photo by CSB Photography

DK
Editor Emma Roberts
Senior Production Editor Jennifer Murray
Senior Production Controller Louise Minihane
Managing Editor Hazel Eriksson
Publishing Director Mark Searle

This American Edition, 2025
Published in the United States by DK Publishing,
a Division of Penguin Random House LLC
1745 Broadway, 20th Floor, New York, NY 10019

25 26 27 28 29 10 9 8 7 6 5 4 3 2 1
001—345793—Dec/2025

Published in Great Britain by Dorling Kindersley Limited.

ISBN 979-8-2171-2612-5

Printed and bound in China

www.dk.com

akidsco.com

This book was made with Forest Stewardship Council™ certified paper—one small step in DK's commitment to a sustainable future. Learn more at **www.dk.com/uk/information/sustainability**

This book is dedicated to my parents, brother, and sister, who teach me about kindness every day.

This book is dedicated to the teachers, mentors (especially Maestro William Henry Curry), friends, and students who taught me that kindness comes in many shapes and sizes.

This book is dedicated to you. You are a shining light in the world. Be kind, be real, be you.

Intro for grownups

We often talk about how peace and love are super important in our world. That's true, but I think there's something else the world needs now, more than ever—kindness.

When I set out to write a book on kindness, I did not know the topic would resonate with so many people. In my family, kindness has always been something you do every day. Now that I'm a grownup, I've realized not everyone is lucky enough to learn how to put kindness into practice from an early age.

Kindness begins at home, and reading this book with the kid in your life is an important step in your journey to building a world where kindness is seen, shown, and felt by everyone. We may not be able to control what happens around us, but we can control our actions and choices. I hope this book will help you and your kid to choose kindness today, tomorrow, the next day, and every day that follows.

WHEN WAS THE LAST TIME SOMEONE MADE YOU SMILE?

Did they say something nice?

Did they give you a handmade card?

Did they tell you a funny joke?

When you feel that warm and fuzzy feeling, that is...

NESS.

Kindness has lots
of different forms, like...

helping,

sharing,

caring,

giving,

and so much more.

It can be words, like:

"YOU ARE MY FRIEND."

"I APPRECIATE YOU."

"I'm grateful for YOU."

"YOU HAVE A NICE SMILE."

"I LOVE YOUR OUTFIT!"

"YOU ARE A VERY GOOD PERSON."

What are kind words to you?

Kindness can be actions, like:

- giving someone a hug or high five
- sharing your toys with someone else
- telling a story or a joke to make someone laugh
- cheering your friend on at their soccer game
- listening while someone talks about their day

What does a kind action look like to you?

There are many different ways to be kind.

And everyone has the supplies to be a kind person. Let me show you!

I like to think about 4 main tools for kindness.

1. SMILES

Everybody's smile is unique
and special, just like snowflakes!

Turn to the person you're reading with
and give them your biggest smile.
Isn't it great to see someone
receiving kindness? I bet
they'll even smile back!

2. WORDS

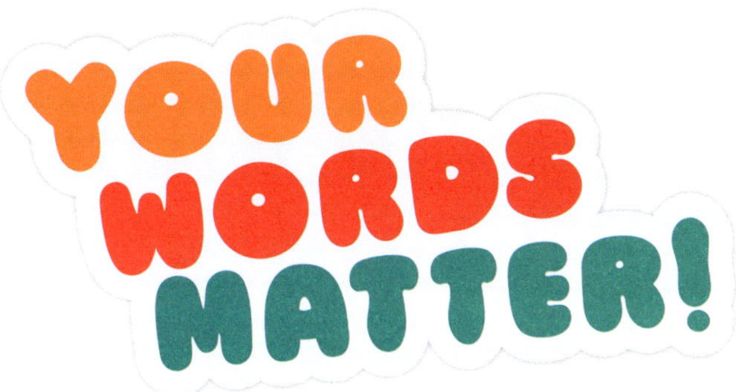

Words are really powerful. They can change a person for better, or for worse. Be kind in choosing your words to make people feel good, not bad.

3. ENERGY

If someone is having a bad day, they might need your energy to make their day brighter. Listening and being present with your friends, family, and classmates is an act of kindness.

4. TIME

Time is the most precious thing we have—even more precious than gold! Spending time with people is one of the most valuable things we can give to one another. Kindness doesn't have to be spoken—it can be seen and felt.

SE

Everyone has the tools to be kind.

BUT...

some people choose not to use them.

KINDNESS IS A CHOICE
WE MAKE EVERY DAY, WITH
EVERYBODY WE MEET.

When you choose kindness, you choose to show other people the joy in supporting one another.

Everyone deserves kindness, no matter who you are, who your family is, how big your home is, what school you go to, or what your hobbies are.

KINDNESS IS FOR EVERYONE. PERIOD.

And that includes being kind to yourself, too.

You can show yourself kindness with the exact same tools you use for everyone else.

GIVE
YOURSELF
A HUG.

TAKE TIME
TO DO
SOMETHING
THAT MAKES
YOU HAPPY.

SMILE
AT YOUR
REFLECTION
IN THE
MIRROR.

And at the end of the day, say,

"THANK YOU
FOR BEING
YOU."

Kindness makes you

STRONGER.

It’s like a muscle that gets bigger the more you use it.

My mom always said, "Do 1 act of kindness for someone every single day." Because when you've done that, it'll have been a good day.*

*And don't forget to make your bed. My mom would want me to say that, too!

This might not feel easy some days, so I like to do a fun exercise to create my kindness before I give it out to others.

LET'S TRY IT TOGETHER!

If you could hold today's kindness in your hands, what shape would it be?

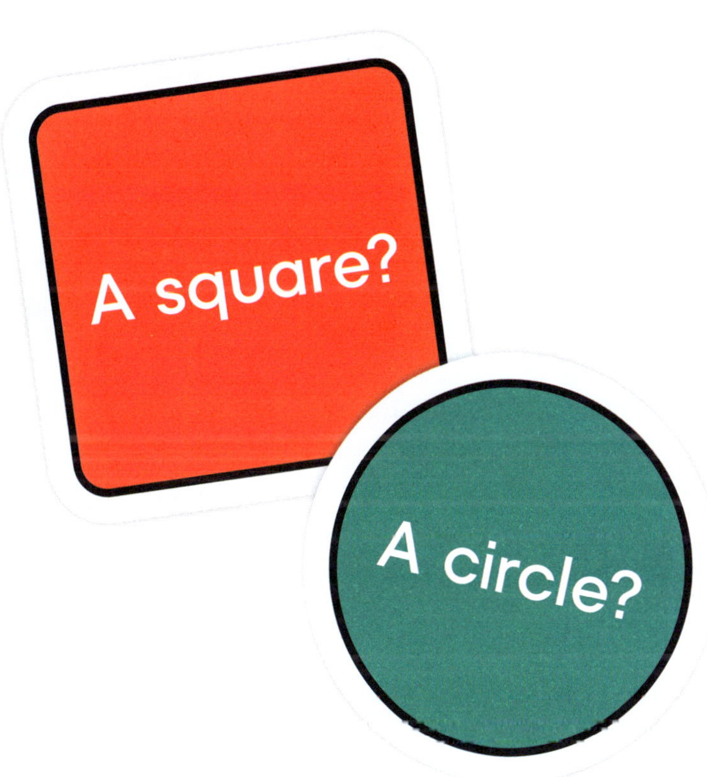
A square?
A circle?

Is it reallyyyyy

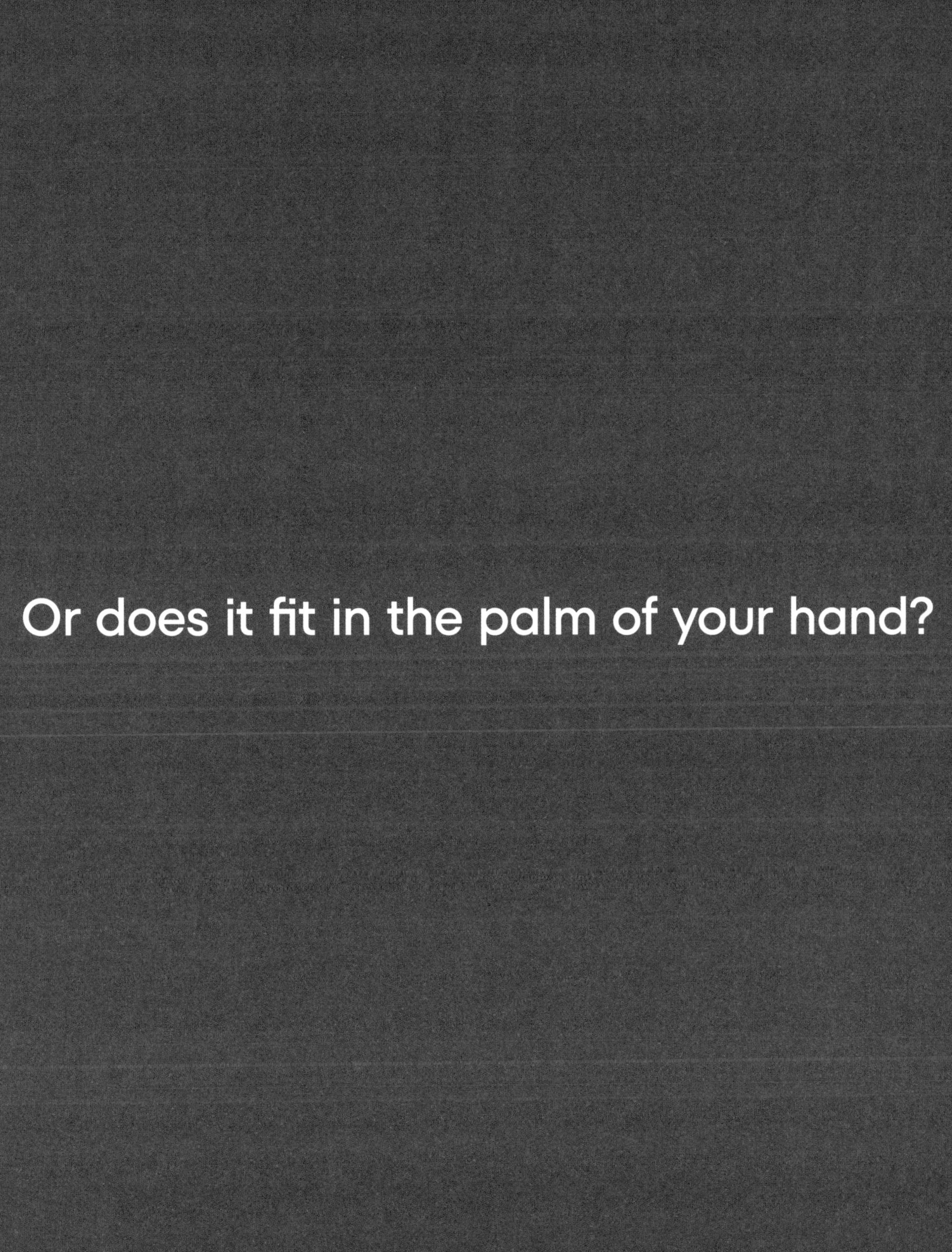
Or does it fit in the palm of your hand?

Is it

TALL?

Is it **SHORT?**

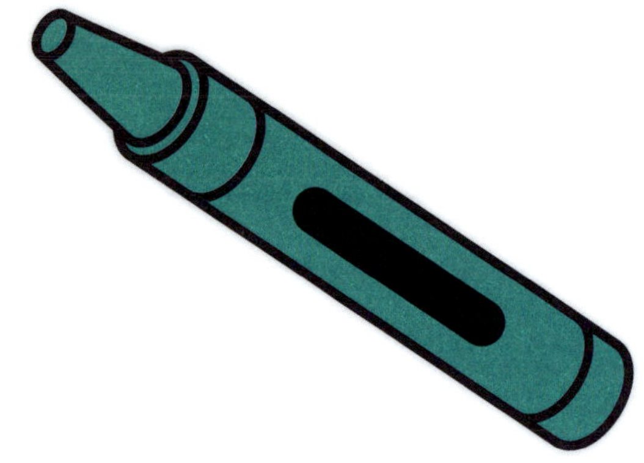

What color is it?
What does it feel like in your heart?

Is it warm and cozy?
Is it strong and powerful?

Is it big and exciting?
Or gentle and comforting, like a hug from your favorite person?

TELL YOUR GROWNUP
ALL ABOUT IT!

And now, go out and give your
kindness to someone else.

The world will be a better place
because you chose kindness today.

I'M SO PROUD OF YOU.

THANK YOU FOR BEING YOU.

Outro
for grownups

The great work has begun. You and your kid are on an exciting journey now. I hope this book has opened your imagination to the possibility of changing people's lives through kindness. Even something as simple as a thank you, a smile, or lending a helping hand can change the way we are as a society. It starts and ends with us all and our choice to put kindness out into the world.

Go out and show everyone the power of being kind. And I bet you will be happily surprised by the kindness you feel in return.

Shine bright. Listen. Show up. Fall down. Get up. Give back. Be you.

About The Author

Jackson Cooper (he/him) has spent his entire life leading with kindness and generosity. Growing up, he felt that kindness could solve the world's problems and dedicated his career and life to giving back through teaching, leading, and mentorship. He's worked for 15+ years in roles with nonprofit and government organizations and will enthusiastically talk about movies, Thai food, running, and career planning at any moment of the day. He teaches at UNC-Greensboro and Seattle University. This is his first book.